20 FUN FACTS ABOUT FAMOUS BRIDGES

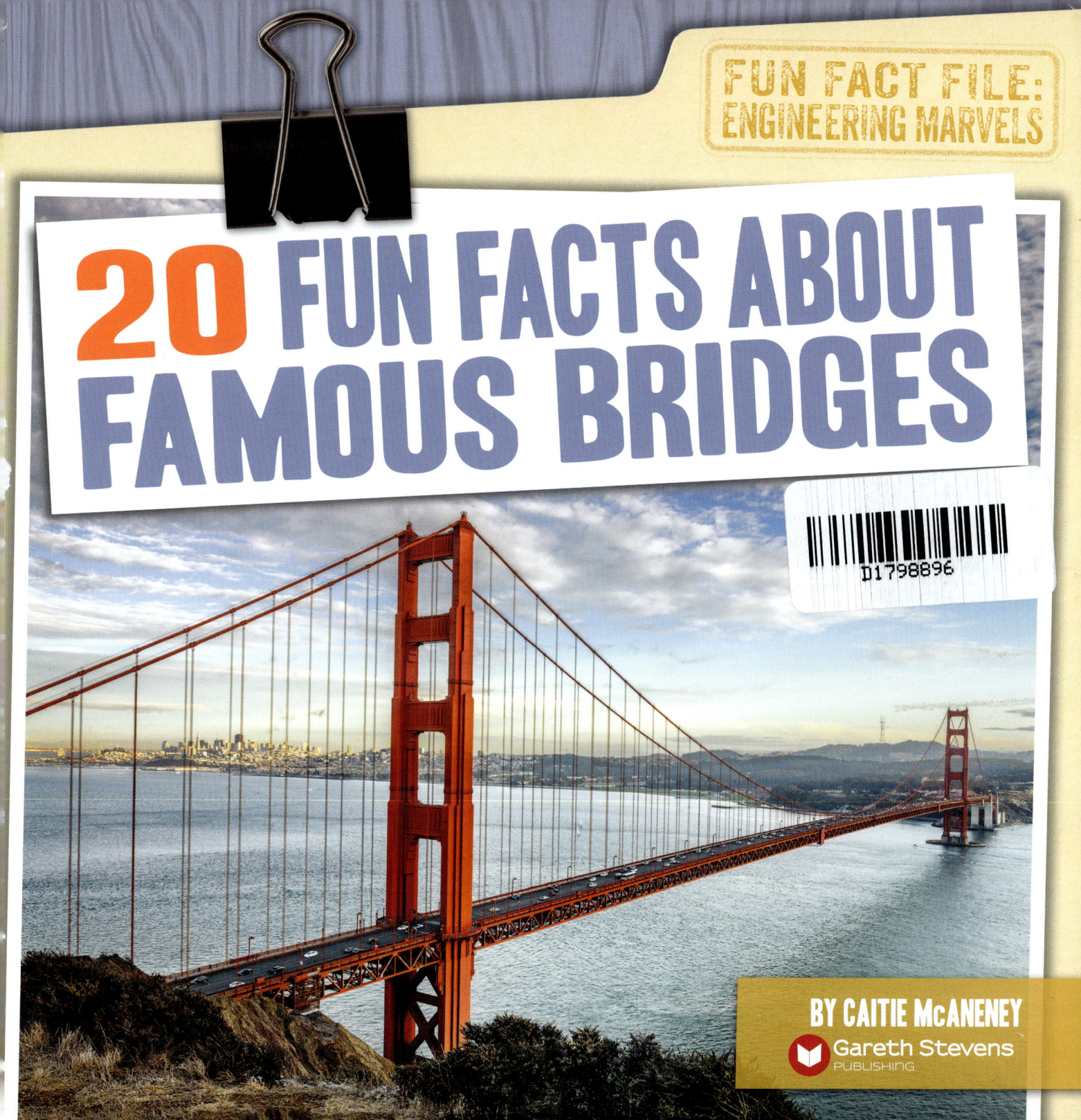

BY CAITIE McANENEY

Gareth Stevens
PUBLISHING

Please visit our website, www.garethstevens.com. For a free color catalog of all our high-quality books, call toll free 1-800-542-2595 or fax 1-877-542-2596.

Library of Congress Cataloging-in-Publication Data

Names: McAneney, Caitie, author.
Title: 20 fun facts about famous bridges / Caitie McAneney.
Other titles: Twenty fun facts about famous bridges
Description: New York : Gareth Stevens Publishing, [2020] | Series: Fun fact file. Engineering marvels
Identifiers: LCCN 2019011452 | ISBN 9781538246504 (pbk.) | ISBN 9781538246528 (library bound) | ISBN 9781538246511 (6 pack)
Subjects: LCSH: Bridges–Miscellanea–Juvenile literature.
Classification: LCC TG148 .M43 2020 | DDC 624.2–dc23
LC record available at https://lccn.loc.gov/2019011452

First Edition

Published in 2020 by
Gareth Stevens Publishing
111 East 14th Street, Suite 349
New York, NY 10003

Designer: Sarah Liddell
Editor: Therese Shea

Photo credits: Cover, p. 1 (main) ventdusud/Shutterstock.com; file folder used throughout David Smart/Shutterstock.com; binder clip used throughout luckyraccoon/Shutterstock.com; wood grain background used throughout ARENA Creative/Shutterstock.com; p. 5 Russ Heinl/Shutterstock.com; p. 6 Flausa123/Wikimedia Commons; pp. 7, 12 Morphart Creation/Shutterstock.com; p. 8 AlexAnton/Shutterstock.com; p. 9 muratart/Shutterstock.com; p. 10 kavram/Shutterstock.com; p. 11 emperorcosar/Shutterstock.com; p. 13 Bettmann/Contributor/Bettmann/Getty Images; p. 14 MGA73bot2/Wikimedia Commons; p. 16 Michael Lawrence Butler/Shutterstock.com; p. 17 Sean Pavone/Shutterstock.com; p. 18 ullstein bild/Contributor/ullstein bild/Getty Images; p. 19 Construction Photography/Avalon/Contributor/Hulton Archive/Getty Images; p. 20 dibrova/Shutterstock.com; p. 21 Ryan Kelehar/Shutterstock.com; p. 22 HelloRF Zcool/Shutterstock.com; p. 23 Nick-D/Shutterstock.com; p. 24 Dan Breckwoldt/Shutterstock.com; p. 25 e2dan/Shutterstock.com; p. 26 Allen.G/Shutterstock.com; p. 27 Sambaloelek/Wikimedia Commons; p. 29 Casper1774 Studio/Shutterstock.com.

Printed in the United States of America

Some of the images in this book illustrate individuals who are models. The depictions do not imply actual situations or events.

CPSIA compliance information: Batch #CW20GS: For further information contact Gareth Stevens, New York, New York at 1-800-542-2595.

CONTENTS

Breathtaking Bridges 4

World's Oldest Bridges 6

Renaissance Bridges 8

Awesome Aqueducts 10

Bridge Disasters! 12

It's a Wonder! 14

The Art of Suspense 16

World's Longest 18

American Marvels 20

Super Sea Bridges 22

Bridges with Views 24

Making Connections 28

Glossary 30

For More Information 31

Index 32

Words in the glossary appear in **bold** type the first time they are used in the text.

BREATHTAKING BRIDGES

Bridges connect places, people, and things. People use them every day! Bridges span, or cross, deep valleys, wide bodies of water, and even tall buildings. Types of bridges include **arch** bridges, suspension bridges, and beam bridges—and each one is a wonder of **engineering**.

Some bridges are hundreds of feet above water or land, and some dip into underwater or underground tunnels. Some bridges have ended in **disaster**, and a few have lasted for thousands of years. Each bridge in this book has a story—and science—behind it.

4

The Confederation Bridge in Canada connects New Brunswick and Prince Edward Island. It's an example of a beam bridge, a type of bridge in which a beam rests on supports, or posts.

WORLD'S OLDEST BRIDGES

THE ARKADIKO BRIDGE IN GREECE IS OVER 3,000 YEARS OLD!

The Arkadiko Bridge in Greece is one of the oldest surviving bridges in the world. It was probably built around 1300 BC! Greeks built this bridge as part of a system of military roads.

Ancient arch bridges like this one were often made of large rocks.

People can still walk over the Arkadiko Bridge and the Caravan Bridge, shown here.

SOME BELIEVE HOMER, SAID TO HAVE WRITTEN THE *ILIAD* AND THE *ODYSSEY*, USED THE CARAVAN BRIDGE!

The Caravan Bridge in Izmir, Turkey, is an arched stone bridge. It was built around 850 BC, about when Homer is said to have lived. So, this bridge is over 2,800 years old!

RENAISSANCE BRIDGES

MANY DIDN'T THINK THE RIALTO BRIDGE OF VENICE, ITALY, WOULD LAST.

The Rialto Bridge was built in the late 1500s over the Grand Canal, the main waterway through Venice. It has no middle support, so many thought it would fall. It's still standing!

The Rialto Bridge was built during the Renaissance period. This was a time when Europeans had new interest in arts and sciences.

FUN FACT: 4

THE PONTE VECCHIO WAS THE ONLY BRIDGE IN FLORENCE, ITALY, THAT THE GERMAN ARMY DIDN'T DESTROY DURING WORLD WAR II (1939–1945).

Completed in 1345, the Ponte Vecchio was the first segmental arch bridge in the western world. Some say German leader Adolf Hitler ordered his soldiers not to harm it.

9

FUN FACT: 5

THE PONT DU GARD AQUEDUCT IN FRANCE IS AN EXAMPLE OF ANCIENT PLUMBING!

Aqueducts are man-made channels for carrying water. They're often tall bridges with pipes. The Pont du Gard was built about 19 BC. It was the highest aqueduct at the time, measuring 155 feet (47 m) high.

10

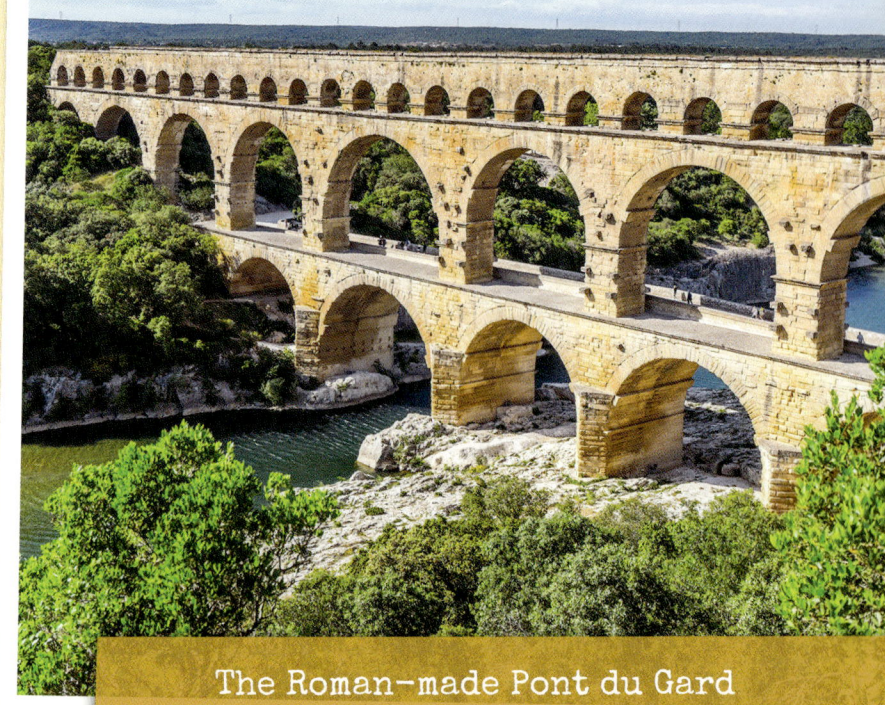

The Roman-made Pont du Gard has many arches that supported a pipe system that brought water to the city of Nîmes.

The Aqueduct of Segovia stands more than 93 feet (28 m) tall.

THE AQUEDUCT OF SEGOVIA IS NEARLY 2,000 YEARS OLD—AND STILL IN USE!

In the first century AD, the Romans built this aqueduct in Spain. It brings water to the city of Segovia from the Frío River. Engineers didn't need to use **mortar** to hold the bridge's 24,000 stone blocks together!

11

BRIDGE DISASTERS!

THE BRIDGE FROM THE SONG "LONDON BRIDGE IS FALLING DOWN" IS REAL!

"London Bridge Is Falling Down" became popular in the 1800s, when New London Bridge was built over the River Thames in England. However, many bridges have been built over the Thames since the 1100s, and some did collapse, or fall down!

12

This picture of London Bridge in the 1600s shows shops and houses built on top of it.

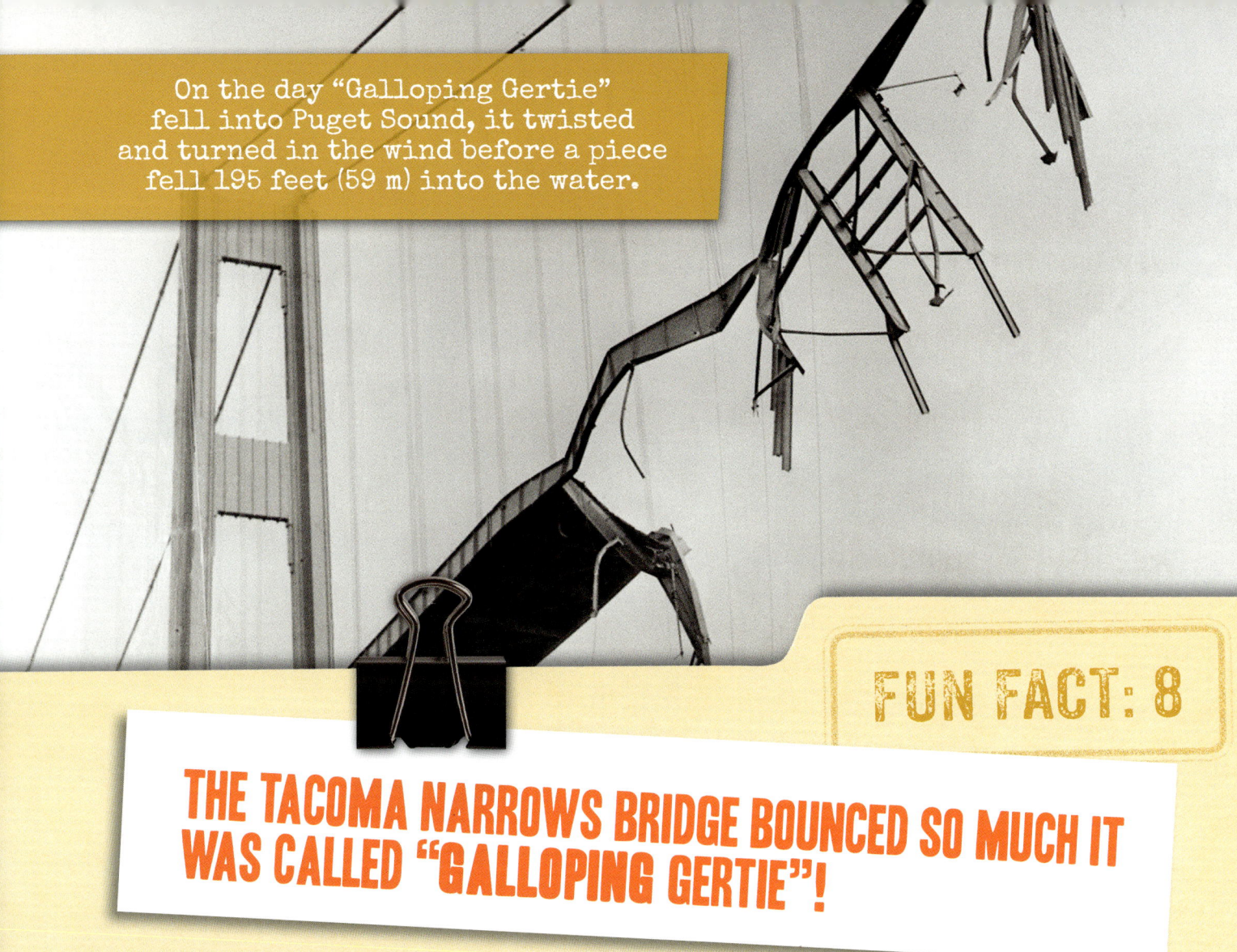

On the day "Galloping Gertie" fell into Puget Sound, it twisted and turned in the wind before a piece fell 195 feet (59 m) into the water.

THE TACOMA NARROWS BRIDGE BOUNCED SO MUCH IT WAS CALLED "GALLOPING GERTIE"!

This bridge in Washington State was a suspension bridge, which means its roadway was supported by cables attached to towers. As workers finished it, they discovered it moved in the wind. On November 7, 1940, it collapsed.

IT'S A WONDER!

THE CHESAPEAKE BAY BRIDGE-TUNNEL IS ONE OF THE "SEVEN ENGINEERING WONDERS OF THE MODERN WORLD"!

Its bridges, tunnels, raised roads, and man-made islands connect Virginia to the **peninsula** that includes the shores of Delaware, Maryland, and Virginia. It's nearly 18 miles (29 km) long!

More than 130 million **vehicles** have used the Chesapeake Bay Bridge-Tunnel. Today, a **parallel** crossing allows for more vehicles.

CHESAPEAKE BAY BRIDGE-TUNNEL

CHESAPEAKE BAY

EASTERN SHORE
OF VIRGINIA

CHESAPEAKE BAY
BRIDGE-TUNNEL

FISHERMAN
ISLAND

MAN-MADE ISLANDS

ATLANTIC OCEAN

VIRGINIA
BEACH

THE ART OF SUSPENSE

WHEN IT WAS BUILT IN 1937, THE GOLDEN GATE BRIDGE WAS THE LONGEST SUSPENSION BRIDGE IN THE WORLD!

The Golden Gate Bridge in San Francisco, California, is almost 2 miles (3.2 km) long. It's still the second-longest suspension bridge in the United States. Only the Verrazano-Narrows Bridge in New York City is longer.

The Golden Gate Bridge is known for its bright color. It was painted "international orange"—a color that makes it stand out.

Japanese engineers had a lot of problems to plan for when they planned the Akashi-Kaikyo Bridge, including **earthquakes** and huge waves called tsunamis!

THE AKASHI-KAIKYO BRIDGE, THE LONGEST SUSPENSION BRIDGE IN THE WORLD, IS NEARLY FOUR TIMES THE LENGTH OF THE BROOKLYN BRIDGE.

The Akashi-Kaikyo Bridge in Japan connects the city of Kōbe, on the island of Honshu, to the city of Iwaya, on the island of Awaji. The bridge is 12,831 feet (3,911 m) long!

17

THE DANYANG-KUNSHAN GRAND BRIDGE IN CHINA IS THE LONGEST BRIDGE IN THE WORLD!

The Danyang-Kunshan Grand Bridge is 102 miles (164 km) long! It's a viaduct, which is a long bridge usually supported by arches or posts that carries a road or railway over water, valleys, or roads.

The Danyang-Kunshan Grand Bridge connects the cities of Shanghai and Nanjing. It carries the Beijing-Shanghai High-Speed Railway.

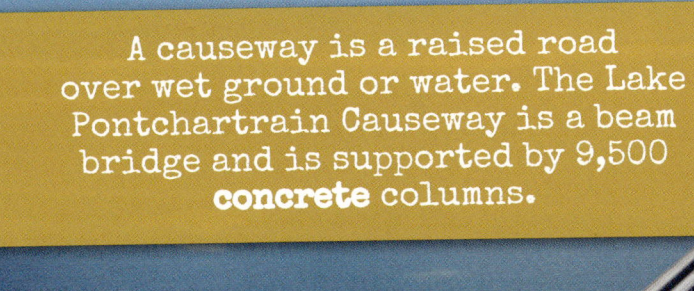

A causeway is a raised road over wet ground or water. The Lake Pontchartrain Causeway is a beam bridge and is supported by 9,500 **concrete** columns.

THE LAKE PONTCHARTRAIN CAUSEWAY IN LOUISIANA IS THE LONGEST BRIDGE IN THE WORLD THAT RUNS CONTINUOUSLY OVER WATER.

Louisiana is home to the Lake Pontchartrain Causeway, two side-by-side bridges. The longer bridge is almost 24 miles (39 km) long. It's continuous, meaning it isn't split into parts, and runs completely over water.

IN 1884, CIRCUS SHOWMAN P. T. BARNUM LED 21 ELEPHANTS OVER THE BROOKLYN BRIDGE.

In 1883, thousands of people were walking on the Brooklyn Bridge. Suddenly, some thought it was going to collapse. Twelve people died as everyone tried to escape. The next year,

When it was completed in 1883, the Brooklyn Bridge was the longest suspension bridge with a main span of 1,595 feet (486 m) long.

20 Barnum's elephants proved the bridge was safe.

The Coronado Bridge, sometimes called the San Diego-Coronado Bay Bridge, is more than 2 miles (3.2 km) long!

CALIFORNIA'S CORONADO BRIDGE WON A PRIZE FOR THE "MOST BEAUTIFUL BRIDGE" IN AMERICA.

Coronado Bridge connects San Diego to the island of Coronado across San Diego Bay. The curving bridge has become a famous sight. Thirty concrete towers support the deck, which stands 200 feet (61 m) above the water.

SUPER SEA BRIDGES

FUN FACT: 16

THE HONG KONG-ZHUHAI-MACAO BRIDGE USES AS MUCH STEEL AS 60 EIFFEL TOWERS!

This bridge is the longest sea bridge. It stretches 34 miles (55 km)! It connects Hong Kong to mainland China. Engineers built the bridge, an undersea tunnel, and two islands to make the crossing possible.

At least 18 people died working on this superlong sea bridge, which opened in 2018.

The Øresund Bridge connects Sweden and Denmark so that people can live and work in both places.

THE ØRESUND BRIDGE ACROSS THE FLINTE CHANNEL IS THE LONGEST COMBINED ROAD AND RAIL BRIDGE IN EUROPE!

The Øresund Bridge carries both vehicles and a railway between Sweden and Denmark. The bridge is about 10 miles (16 km) long and connects to a man-made island and a tunnel.

BRIDGES WITH VIEWS

YOU CAN CLIMB THE SYDNEY HARBOUR BRIDGE FOR THE BEST VIEW IN SYDNEY, AUSTRALIA!

The Sydney Harbour Bridge is the largest steel arch bridge on Earth. It allows cars, bicycles, trains, and walkers to cross into Sydney. If you're brave, you can climb its arch!

Sydney is the largest city in Australia. Its landmarks, or famous features, include the Sydney Opera House and the Sydney Harbour Bridge, both pictured here.

Victoria Falls in Africa is twice as high and twice as wide as Niagara Falls. The Victoria Falls Bridge offers an amazing view of it.

PEOPLE BUNGEE JUMP FROM THE VICTORIA FALLS BRIDGE IN AFRICA!

The Victoria Falls Bridge crosses the Zambezi River, between the countries of Zambia and Zimbabwe. When it opened in 1905, the bridge was the highest in the world at 420 feet (128 m) off the ground.

Benson Bridge provides an up-close view of Multnomah Falls!

MORE THAN 2 MILLION PEOPLE VISIT THE BENSON BRIDGE IN OREGON EACH YEAR!

Multnomah Falls is a popular natural landmark in Oregon. The 635-foot (194 m) waterfall is the tallest in the state. People can walk 100 feet (30 m) above the lower pool by crossing Benson Bridge on foot.

LANDMARK BRIDGES IN NORTH AMERICA

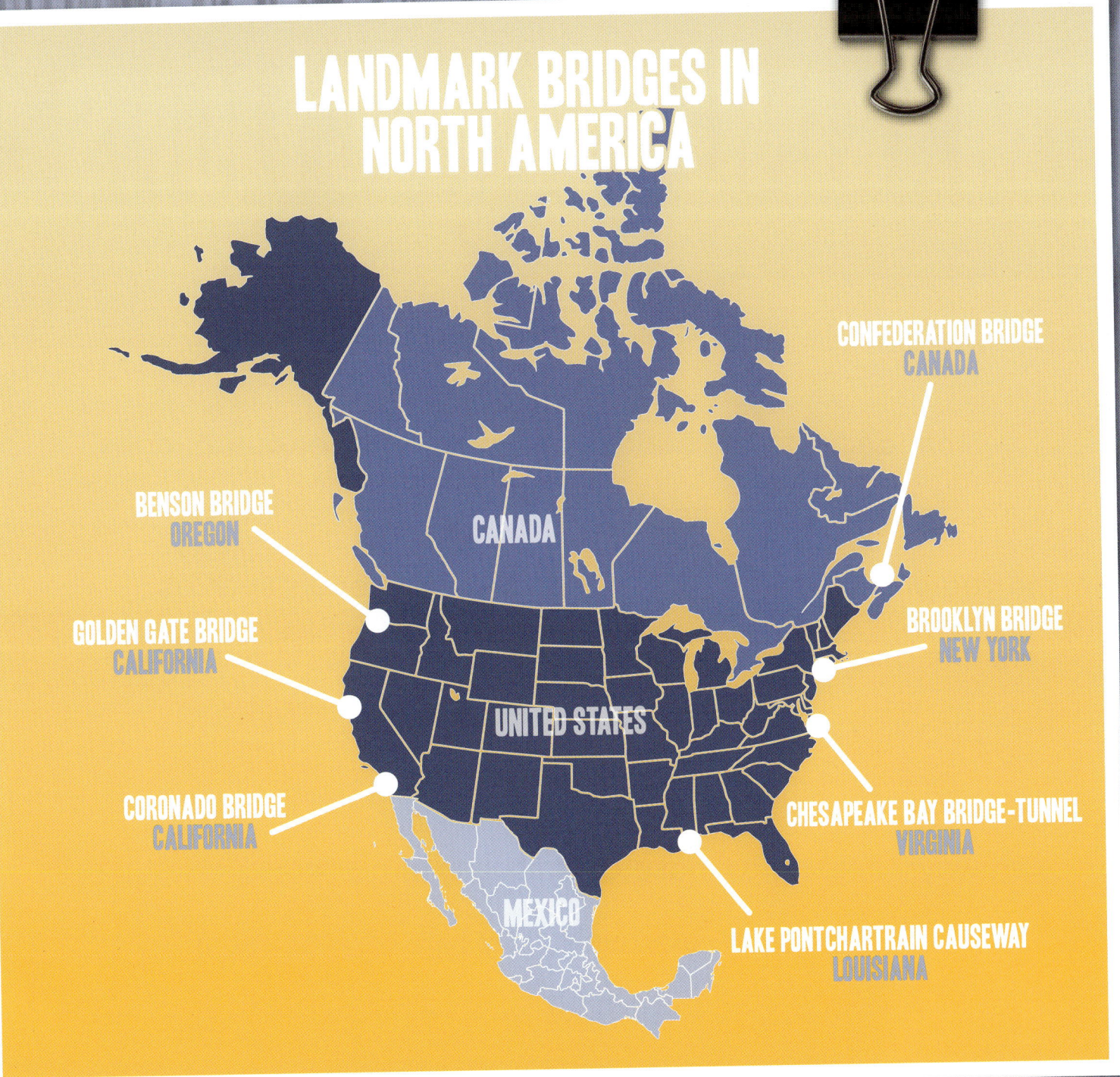

CONFEDERATION BRIDGE
CANADA

BENSON BRIDGE
OREGON

CANADA

GOLDEN GATE BRIDGE
CALIFORNIA

BROOKLYN BRIDGE
NEW YORK

UNITED STATES

CORONADO BRIDGE
CALIFORNIA

CHESAPEAKE BAY BRIDGE-TUNNEL
VIRGINIA

MEXICO

LAKE PONTCHARTRAIN CAUSEWAY
LOUISIANA

MAKING CONNECTIONS

From ancient arch bridges to modern suspension bridges, you've read and seen how bridges have changed over the years. Engineers of today use strong materials such as concrete and steel and clever designs, or plans, to make sure bridges will last—and look good!

However, all bridges are engineering marvels in their own ways, helping us make connections in our world. Whether we're walking, driving, or traveling by rail, bridges often help us get where we need to go. Our world wouldn't be the same without bridges!

Many bridges built today combine beauty and engineering, such as the Helix Bridge in Singapore, shown here.

GLOSSARY

arch: a structure built in the shape of a curve

bungee jump: to jump from a very high place while attached to a long rope that stretches and keeps you from hitting the ground

concrete: a hard, strong material used for building and made by mixing cement, sand, and broken rocks with water

disaster: an event that causes much suffering or loss

earthquake: a shaking of the ground caused by the movement of Earth's crust

engineering: the use of science and math to build better objects

galloping: describing the fastest running movement for a horse

mortar: a wet matter spread between bricks or stones that holds them together when it hardens

parallel: laying in the same direction as another thing

peninsula: a narrow piece of land that extends into water from the mainland

plumbing: a system of pipes that carries water through a building

vehicle: an object used for carrying or transporting people or goods, such as a car, truck, or airplane

FOR MORE INFORMATION

BOOKS

Marsico, Katie. *Bridges.* New York, NY: Children's Press, 2016.

Stine, Megan. *Where Is the Brooklyn Bridge?* New York, NY: Grosset & Dunlap, 2016.

WEBSITES

All About Bridges

easyscienceforkids.com/all-about-bridges/
Learn about the science behind bridges and how different types of bridges are used today.

Engineering Facts—Bridge Facts

www.sciencekids.co.nz/sciencefacts/engineering/bridges.html
Want more fun facts about bridges? Check out this webpage!

Golden Gate Bridge Facts for Kids

kidzfeed.com/golden-gate-bridge-facts-for-kids/
Check out more fun facts about the Golden Gate Bridge!

INDEX

Akashi-Kaikyo Bridge 17

Aqueduct of Segovia 11

aqueducts 10, 11

arch bridge 4, 6, 28

Arkadiko Bridge 6, 7

Barnum, P. T. 20

beam bridge 4, 5, 19

Benson Bridge 26

Brooklyn Bridge 17, 20

Caravan Bridge 7

causeway 19

Chesapeake Bay Bridge-Tunnel 14

Confederation Bridge 5

Coronado Bridge 21

Danyang-Kunshan Grand Bridge 18

engineers 11, 17, 22, 28

Golden Gate Bridge 16

Greece 6

Homer 7

Hong Kong-Zhuhai-Macao 22

Italy 8, 9

New London Bridge 12

Pontchartrain Causeway 19

Pont du Gard 10

Ponte Vecchio 9

railway 18, 23

Renaissance 8

Rialto Bridge 8

River Thames 12

segmental arch bridge 9

steel arch bridge 24

suspension bridge 13, 16, 17, 20

Sydney Harbour Bridge 24

Tacoma Narrows Bridge ("Galloping Gertie") 13

valleys 4, 18

viaduct 18

Victoria Falls Bridge 25

World War II 9

Øresund Bridge 23